SUSTAINABLE SAFETY LEADERSHIP
WORKBOOK

Sustainable Safety Leadership

Workbook

TONY E MEDLEY

MEDLEY
PUBLISHING GROUP

First Printing, 2025

ISBN: 979-8-9934305-4-6
Cover Design: T.E. Medley
Interior Design: T.E. Medley
Published by: Medley Publishing Group

This workbook is intended for educational and professional development purposes. It is not a substitute for legal, compliance, or safety-regulatory counsel. Leadership teams should consult applicable organizational policies and state/federal regulations when implementing any strategies or tools contained herein.

Printed in the United States of America.

CONTENTS

INTRODUCTION

This workbook is a leadership tool designed to move Sustainable Safety from concept to action. Each section aligns directly with the book's chapters and provides:

- Strategic planning worksheets
- Reflective leadership questions
- Implementation templates
- Key performance tracking tools

Use this workbook during leadership retreats, executive planning sessions, or ongoing safety-improvement initiatives. Treat each chapter not as theory, but as a strategic workshop.

Workbook Structure

Each workbook chapter includes:

- Chapter Summary & Key Insights
- Leadership Reflection
- Discussion Questions
- Strategic Planning Exercises
- Action Tools & Templates
- Key Metrics & Accountability Notes

| 1 |

The Evolution of Safety Thinking

OBJECTIVE

Understand how safety philosophy evolved and identify where your organization stands.

Reflection Questions

- How has our safety culture historically evolved?

- What stage of maturity best describes our current approach: compliance, control, engagement, or sustainability?

- What lessons from past incidents have reshaped our priorities?

Exercise: The Safety Timeline

Draw a timeline of major milestones, cultural shifts, and turning points in your organization's safety journey. Mark where we've been, where we are, and where we aim to be.

Action Tool

Define your organization's current Safety Culture Phase:

1. Reactive:

2. Proactive:

3. Predictive:

4. Generative:

| 2 |

Why Sustainability Matters in Safety

Objective

Identify the long-term business and moral case for sustaining safety.

Reflection Questions

- What would "safety sustainability" mean in our specific industry context?

- Which areas of our safety performance are cyclical rather than continuous?

- How do our leadership practices encourage short-term results instead of long-term resilience?

Exercise: Safety Sustainability SWOT Analysis

Complete a Safety Sustainability SWOT Analysis by identifying:

- Strengths

- Weaknesses

- Opportunities

- Threats

Use this analysis to evaluate what supports or challenges long-term safety improvement.

Action Tool

Draft a one-paragraph Safety Sustainability Statement suitable for inclusion in your corporate mission, values charter, or long-range strategy.

| 3 |

The Role of Leadership in Sustained Engagement

Objective

Define how leadership behaviors drive engagement and accountability.

Reflection Questions

- What visible actions demonstrate my personal commitment to safety?

- How do I reinforce trust and ownership among my team?

- Do I measure engagement or only compliance?

Exercise: Leadership Touchpoints

List your top five leadership touchpoints for influencing safety daily. Examples may include field visits, team huddles, coaching moments, or review sessions.

Action Tool

Create a **Leadership Engagement Calendar** outlining your weekly, monthly, and quarterly touchpoints that drive sustained engagement and accountability.

| 4 |

Beyond Compliance

The Strategic Purpose of Safety Metrics

Objective

Redefine measurement as insight, not inspection.

Reflection Questions

- Which of our current metrics drive genuine improvement?

- What key information is missing from our performance dashboards?

- How can we create a healthy balance between lagging and leading indicators?

Exercise: Leadership Dashboard Prototype

Design a prototype dashboard that includes a blend of:

- Outcome measures
- Behavioral indicators
- Cultural insights

Use this exercise to imagine how a more balanced and meaningful measurement system could guide leadership decisions.

Action Tool

Draft your top five Strategic Metrics of Meaning, ensuring each one aligns directly with your organization's mission, values, and long-term safety goals.

| 5 |

The Anatomy of a Leading Indicator

Objective

Build metrics that predict and influence outcomes.

Reflection Questions

- What indicators show early warning of risk?

- How do we ensure our indicators measure quality, not just quantity?

Exercise: Leading Indicator Design Canvas

Work through the components of a Leading Indicator using the following prompts:

- Define the behavior.

- Set clear measurement criteria.

- Identify data sources.

- Establish ownership.

- Set the frequency and review cycle.

Use this canvas to intentionally design indicators that guide proactive decision-making.

Action Tool

Select three new leading indicators to pilot over the next 90 days. Document why you chose them, how they will be tracked, and what success will look like.

| 6 |

Designing Effective Safety KPIs

Objective

Align KPIs with both leadership performance and employee behavior.

Reflection Questions

- How do our KPIs connect to strategic business priorities?

- Are our KPIs clear, measurable, and motivating?

Exercise: KPI Redesign Using SMART-S

Redesign the KPIs for one department using the SMART-S Framework:

- Specific

- Measurable

- Achievable

- Relevant

- Time-Bound

- Sustainable

Use this exercise to ensure each KPI supports both operational excellence and long-term cultural improvement.

Action Tool

Create a one-page KPI Summary Sheet that links each metric to its corresponding leadership behavior. This summary should make it easy to see how measurement aligns with daily leadership actions.

| 7 |

Data to Dialogue

Translating Metrics into Meaningful Action

Objective

Improve communication of performance data.

Reflection Questions

- Do our reports inspire action or simply record history?

- How often do metrics lead to real conversation, coaching, or problem-solving?

Exercise: Safety Communication Audit

Conduct a Safety Communication Audit by reviewing recent:

- Reports
- Leadership meetings
- Dashboards
- Briefings or summaries

Evaluate each for clarity, usefulness, and engagement.

Identify where information is clear, where it is confusing, and where communication fails to drive action.

Action Tool

Develop a Monthly "Metrics to Meaning" Conversation Template for leadership reviews. This template should guide leaders in turning data into dialogue by focusing on:

- What the numbers actually mean?
- What behaviors contributed to the results?
- What strategic actions are needed next?
- What follow-up or coaching is required?

Observations, Near Misses, Coaching Conversations

Objective

Strengthen learning through open observation and feedback.

Reflection Questions

- How do we treat near misses— as warnings or as inconveniences?

- How confident are employees in reporting unsafe conditions?

- What patterns emerge from recent observations or reports?

Exercise: Coaching Conversations Practice

Conduct **five coaching conversations** using the *Observe – Ask – Affirm – Advise* model. Use each step intentionally:

- **Observe:** Describe what you see without judgment.
- **Ask:** Invite the employee to share perspective and reasoning.
- **Affirm:** Reinforce positive behaviors and intentions.

- **Advise:** Provide clear guidance or corrective action when needed.

Action Tool

Implement a Near Miss Response Tracker that emphasizes:

- Timely reporting
- Clear follow-up
- Closure of corrective actions
- Feedback loops from leadership back to employees

Use this tool to strengthen psychological safety, transparency, and shared accountability.

| 9 |

Training, Auditing & Continuous Improvement Loops

Objective

Create learning systems that evolve with time.

Reflection Questions

- Do our audits uncover meaningful gaps or merely confirm compliance?

- How do we translate audit findings into true learning actions?

- Where do our current training and auditing processes fail to reinforce long-term improvement?

Exercise: Continuous Improvement Loop Mapping

Map a Continuous Improvement Loop using the following stages:

- Audit
- Analyze
- Act

- Assess
- Adjust

Use this sequence to visualize how information should flow through your organization and where breakdowns may occur.

Action Tool

Build a Safety Training Evaluation Matrix that assesses:

- Content Relevance
- Delivery Quality
- Behavior Change
- Business Impact

Use this matrix to evaluate existing training programs and identify opportunities for improvement and alignment with organizational goals.

| 10 |

The Rotating Leadership Model

Objective

Establish shared ownership through structured leadership rotation.

Reflection Questions

- How can we engage all leaders without diluting accountability?

- What benefits would a rotational focus bring to our culture?

- Which leadership behaviors need broader participation across the team?

Exercise: 12-Month Leadership Rotation Plan

Develop a 12-Month Leadership Rotation Plan by assigning monthly safety themes or priorities to different leaders. Examples of monthly focus areas might include:

- Observations

- Near Miss Review

- Training Quality

- Coaching Conversations

- Safety Metrics Review

- Continuous Improvement Initiatives

Use this exercise to create predictable cycles of ownership and visibility.

Action Tool

Create a Rotation Tracker that includes:

- Leadership roles

- Monthly focus areas

- Key actions

- Feedback cycles

- Completion notes

This tool helps ensure consistency, accountability, and transparent follow-up throughout the rotation.

| 11 |

The Architecture of Engagement

Sustaining Employee Involvement and Ownership

Objective

Sustain employee ownership through intentional design and empowerment.

Reflection Questions

- What barriers prevent full engagement?

- How do we celebrate and reinforce participation?

- Which engagement channels are underused or missing?

Exercise: Engagement Architecture Mapping

Map your organization's Engagement Architecture by identifying and evaluating:

- Formal committees
- Peer networks
- Recognition systems
- Communication channels
- Feedback loops
- Employee-led forums or initiatives

Use this map to understand where engagement is strong, where it is weak, and where structural improvements can be made.

Action Tool

Launch one Employee-Driven Improvement Initiative this quarter. Focus on an initiative that:

- Addresses a real need
- Gives employees visible ownership
- Reinforces shared accountability
- Creates momentum for sustained engagement

| 12 |

The Science of Motivation

How to Keep Safety Energy Alive Over Time

Objective

Maintain safety enthusiasm through intrinsic motivation.

Reflection Questions

- What motivates people most in our workplace—recognition, autonomy, or belonging?

- How can leaders maintain motivation after campaigns or initiatives end?

- Where do we unintentionally weaken or discourage natural motivation?

Exercise: The 3D Motivation Audit

Apply the 3D Motivation Audit to assess your team's morale:

- **Drive:** What energizes people to take action?

- **Direction:** Are people clear about priorities and expectations?

- **Duration:** How long does motivation last before it fades?

Use this audit to identify strengths and gaps in your motivation strategy.

Action Tool

Build a **Sustainable Motivation Plan** that integrates:

- Recognition strategies
- Refresher activities
- Renewal practices such as developmental opportunities or cross-team engagement

This plan should help maintain long-term enthusiasm, ownership, and safety excellence.

| 13 |

Building a Resilient Safety Culture

Adapting to Change and Challenge

Objective

Prepare teams to adapt to disruption without losing commitment.

Reflection Questions

- What lessons have we learned from past crises or major changes?

- How do we model resilience as leaders?

- What behaviors or systems help us remain steady during uncertainty?

Exercise: Crisis-Readiness Playbook

Create a Crisis-Readiness Playbook that outlines:

- Decision-making roles

- Communication flows

- Resource triggers

- Escalation pathways

- Stabilization steps

Use this playbook to clarify how your team responds before, during, and after a disruptive event.

Action Tool

Establish a Resilience Indicator Dashboard that tracks:

- Preparedness levels
- Response time
- Recovery rate
- Team morale

This dashboard helps leaders assess resilience patterns and identify areas needing reinforcement.

| 14 |

Leading Through Crisis

The Safety Professional as Strategic Stabilizer

Objective

Develop a calm, coordinated leadership response.

Reflection Questions

- How prepared are we—emotionally and structurally—for high-stress events?

- Do we have a defined *stabilizer team* or decision cell?

- What gaps in our current response model become visible under pressure?

Exercise: Crisis Simulation Using the OODA Leadership Loop

Simulate a crisis event using the OODA Leadership Loop:

- Observe

- Orient

- Decide

- Act

Use this simulation to test clarity, speed, and alignment during critical moments.

Action Tool

Develop a Crisis Leadership Charter that defines:

- Roles and responsibilities

- Decision authority

- Communication frequency and channels

- Expectations during activation

- Debrief and recovery protocols

This charter establishes a stabilized leadership framework during periods of disruption.

| 15 |

Safety and Strategic Influence

*Positioning the Safety Function at the Leadership
Table*

Objective

Position safety at the leadership table.

Reflection Questions

- How is safety integrated into our strategic planning process?

- What business value can we clearly demonstrate?

- How effectively do we communicate safety in terms leaders understand (risk, cost, impact, productivity)?

Exercise: Safety Strategy Briefing Deck

Prepare a Safety Strategy Briefing Deck that uses business language such as:

- Return on Investment (ROI)

- Productivity impact

- Operational efficiency

- Financial risk reduction

- Brand reputation and trust

Use this exercise to translate safety initiatives into executive-level strategic value.

Action Tool

Create a Safety Business Case Template leaders can use to justify:

- New initiatives
- Resource allocation
- Technology or equipment investments
- Training and capability development
- Long-term cultural improvements

This template should clearly connect safety actions to organizational performance and measurable outcomes.

| 16 |

Integrating Technology and Human Performance

The Future of Sustainable Safety

Objective

Balance digital innovation with human factors.

Reflection Questions

- Which technologies could enhance—not replace—human decision-making?

- How do we manage data ethics, privacy, and employee trust?

- Where might digital tools unintentionally create new risks?

Exercise: Human–Technology Interface Mapping

Map the Human–Technology Interface in your operations and identify three opportunities for safer, more thoughtful integration. Consider areas such as:

- Automation
- Wearables or sensors
- Data dashboards
- AI-assisted decision tools
- Communication platforms
- Training technologies

Use this exercise to highlight where technology strengthens—or weakens—safety performance.

Action Tool

Establish a **Digital Ethics Checklist** for all new safety technologies, addressing:

- Transparency

- Data ownership

- Privacy protections

- Bias or error risks

- User experience

- Oversight and accountability

This checklist ensures digital tools support your people, values, and long-term safety culture.

| 17 |

Global Trends

Future Landscape of Safety Leadership

bjective

Prepare for emerging global forces.

Reflection Questions

- How will ESG and sustainability standards reshape safety expectations?

- What global risks—economic, environmental, technological, or geopolitical—could disrupt our operations?

- Which long-term trends require leadership attention today?

Exercise: Future Scenario Planning Workshop

Conduct a Future Scenario Planning Workshop using three time horizons:

- **3 years:** near-term pressures, regulatory shifts, workforce expectations

- **10 years:** industry transformation, technology evolution, cultural changes

- **25 years:** global forces, megatrends, environmental and economic disruptions

Use these horizons to test assumptions, explore possibilities, and identify strategic safety implications.

Action Tool

Build a **Global Risk Readiness Index** for your enterprise by assessing:

- Vulnerabilities
- Strengths
- Adaptive capacity
- Resource availability
- Crisis recovery capability

This index helps leaders evaluate preparedness for emerging global challenges.

| 18 |

The Legacy of Leadership

Embedding Sustainable Safety for Generations to Come

Objective

Embed safety into the organization's DNA.

Reflection Questions

- What legacy will my leadership leave?

- How am I mentoring the next generation of safety leaders?

- Which leadership habits today will shape safety culture long after I'm gone?

Exercise: Leadership Legacy Statement

Write your personal Leadership Legacy Statement, describing the long-term impact you intend to have on safety culture.
Consider your:

- Values

- Behaviors

- Influence

- Decision-making

- Mentorship impact

- Cultural contributions

Use this statement to guide intentional leadership choices.

Action Tool

Create a Mentorship Plan that pairs emerging leaders with experienced mentors. Include:

- Roles and expectations

- Meeting frequency

- Development goals

- Skill-building focus areas

- Feedback and evaluation methods

This plan helps ensure leadership strength is continually renewed.

| 19 |

Measuring the Unseen

Assessing the True Impact of a Sustainable Safety Culture

Objective

Quantify culture, trust, and engagement.

Reflection Questions

- What metrics could reflect the human side of safety?

- Are our data-gathering methods ethical, transparent, and respectful?

- How do we ensure people feel safe providing honest feedback?

Exercise: Safety Culture Index (SCI) Design

Design a Safety Culture Index (SCI) by combining metrics that reflect:

- Engagement

- Trust

- Learning behavior

- Psychological safety

- Peer accountability

- Leadership credibility

Use this exercise to create a meaningful, holistic view of your organization's cultural health.

Action Tool

Schedule quarterly Culture Health Checks using:

- Surveys
- Focus groups
- Listening sessions
- Debrief meetings

Use the results to guide leadership actions, improve communication, and strengthen cultural resilience.

| 20 |

The Safety Legacy Blueprint

Frameworks for Future-Ready Organizations

Objective

Build a lasting framework for sustainable safety.

Reflection Questions

- Are our systems aligned for long-term resilience?

- Do we have clear mechanisms for renewal and adaptation?

- What elements of our safety culture are most likely to endure—and which may fade without support?

Exercise: Safety Legacy Framework Canvas

Develop a Safety Legacy Framework Canvas that covers five pillars:

- **Purpose** – Why safety exists at the center of your mission

- **People** – How teams, leaders, and partnerships strengthen safety

- **Process** – The systems, routines, and standards that maintain performance

- **Performance** – The outcomes and metrics that define long-term success

- **Renewal** – The practices that ensure continuous learning and adaptation

Use this canvas to design a safety legacy that can withstand change and evolve with time.

Action Tool

Conduct an **Annual Framework Health Audit** using the blueprint model. Evaluate:

- Strengths
- Gaps
- Resource needs
- Cultural readiness
- Alignment with strategic goals

This audit ensures your safety legacy remains strong, relevant, and sustainable year after year.